MY BAB.

MY BREASTS

MY BEST

Pregnancy, birth, breastfeeding and life

as a first time mum.

Vanessa Coulthard

MY BABY

MY BREASTS

MY BEST

Pregnancy, birth, breastfeeding and life as a first
time mum.

Copyright © 2022 by Vanessa Coulthard

Self-published by MrsVanessa Coulthard

Illustrated by Mr A T Selvakumaran

First edition published 2022

This is a memoir. The events are portrayed to the best of my memory. While all the stories in
this book are true, some names and identifying details have been changed to protect the
privacy   of   the   people   involved.

MY BABY

MY BREASTS

MY BEST

First edition published 2022

Me before my baby   8

Being pregnant   15

Meeting Mia for the first time   41

Breastfeeding   52

Seeing the light at the end of the tunnel   61

Life changes for more than the baby and the mum   87

Summary of golden tips   94

Acknowledgments   98

References   101

So here I am, sitting on my rocking chair in our living room after arriving from the hospital with stitches in my abdomen, an incontinence diaper on, excruciating pain in my breasts, a very hungry baby in my arms and tears start running down my cheeks.

Let's find out how I got here...

Before you start reading this book, you have to understand there is nothing or no one in this world I love more than my daughter, that I really wanted to get pregnant and was lucky enough to do so quickly. Please read through my experience until the end and, whatever you do, please do not think I am ungrateful for having the great honour of being a mother and therefore having the opportunity to breastfeed my baby and watch her grow every day.

My baby Mia is the most precious gift I have ever received and I don't understand how I ever felt my life was full before having her.

I sincerely feel for those women who would give anything to know what breastfeeding feels like but can't. Either because they can't conceive or have other problems, due to medical issues, or simply the pain is just unbearable to them.

However, I am not going to sugarcoat it. I will not romanticise the idea of breastfeeding because for me, breastfeeding was ten times worse than recovering from my C-Section. The good news is it does not have to hurt like this.

Those who know me are aware I am not the most positive person in the world but also not the most negative one either. I would rather describe myself as a realist. I like to see things for what they are and to hear the truth, even if it hurts. I believe both positive and pessimistic people should know all the facts so they can then arrive at whatever conclusion they see fit.

The aim of this book is not to put you off breastfeeding nor encourage you to do so, there is enough pressure out there already. I wouldn't dare try to persuade you one way or the other because it happened to me whilst I was pregnant, and I hated it. In this, there is no golden rule, we are all different people and what is good or possible for me, might not be for you and vice versa.

It is, however, a means by which I can tell you the truth, **my truth,** which may or may not be different to others you will live through or hear from friends and family. But, I believe many important things are left unsaid and whilst they are hard to say, they should be spoken of. The trouble is, hardly anyone ever does.

The core of this memoir began a long time ago without me even knowing it. A friend of mine was struggling with breastfeeding and I gave her every tip I had learned whilst going through it myself. Then another one, and another one... before I knew it I had drafted a short page summarising what I had learned and it helped them.

I am no expert but I can tell you about my experience and I promise I will tell you about every single trick I learned and used to ease the pain I felt whilst breastfeeding. I hope that when you finish reading this book you are empowered to put these tips into practice and they work for you as they did for me. If for any reason they don't, please remember it is ok too. After all, we are all wired differently and thresholds of pain are not the same for everyone.

Just remember, it is your baby, your breasts and all you can do is your best.

Finally, it is not the intention of this book to either criticise or praise the medical services rendered to me during the most critical moments of my experience.

I truly believe that the counselling and advice provided by the healthcare professionals are based on established guidelines and/or honoured traditions. However, while being presented to me in good faith, some of these recommendations were not conducive to my well-being.

I would therefore like to extend my most sincere apologies to anyone who may feel offended by the details of this true story.

Me before my baby

Before I start telling you about my pregnancy experience, becoming a mother and breastfeeding, I want to reiterate I am not a midwife nor did I have experience in terms of maternal care. I don't have any cousins or older sisters and prior to pregnancy, my exposure to babies and children was very limited and I didn't have any friends closeby with kids.

I was probably just like many women who know they want to be mothers and idolise the idea of it. Whilst they know it is hard they have no idea how hard; they just know they want it so bad and that is enough to go blind and jump in the pool.

Back when I was 15, I always thought I would get married at 25 and have my first kid at 27, HA!!! Didn't really work like that and thank God. By the time I reached the age by which years ago I thought I would be getting married, I realised how immature I was and not even close to being ready to get married, let alone have children.

There were still a thousand things I wanted to do before getting so serious, like travelling, partying, going to festivals, hanging out with friends and just living without any other responsibility other than myself which is in itself a huge task.

When I turned 25 I had moved from Venezuela to the United Kingdom where I got my first job fresh out of University. This job allowed me to meet people and create my own bubble of friends which became my family abroad.

Spending time with them was the most important thing. I had just ended a long term relationship and I was not looking for anything or anyone new. I just wanted to be single and learn to be happy with myself, which took more years than I expected but, cliche or not, everything happens for a reason. I really believe I simply was not open to the idea of fulfilling the timeline I had set for myself years ago. If I had, I sincerely believe it would have been the perfect recipe for disaster.

Nothing ever happens as you expect and today I am very thankful for that. By the time I was 31 I ended up falling in love with my best friend at an age when I had done all I wanted so I was ready to give myself completely.

I met José through my first job in London in 2011 and he was married at the time so there was no romantic connection between us whatsoever. We became really good friends and we knew everything about each other.

We were already very close friends before, but after he divorced in 2014 we became even closer. He was a huge support to me when I arrived in the UK and I would like to think I was the same for him after his whole world suddenly changed.

Every week our group of friends would gather for drinks after work and during weekends. So José and I really spent a lot of time together. Even my dad used to joke about him being in every picture I posted on social media.

We also travelled a lot before becoming a couple so there is really not much we didn't know about each other. Together with other friends we travelled to Bath, Marbella, Porto, Barcelona and Paris and all of these trips hold a very special place in my heart because they were a lot of fun and exactly what I wanted to do whilst I was single.

At some point I started noticing his "friend vibe" was changing a bit. For a good year, our friends would tell me he was mad about me and I would just say they were wrong and that we were best friends and he cared for me a lot.

When he finally made a move, and I understood our friends were right, I panicked a bit. I didn't want to ruin our friendship, he was too important to me and I didn't want to lose him if things didn't turn out alright.

Eventually he stopped trying and started dating other people and that is exactly when it hit me. I didn't want to be with him, but I also didn't want him to be with anyone else either. I never felt like this in the past with José. Before, we would even discuss the people we liked, our crushes, talk about our dates and it was normal. I never before felt jealousy towards him and this is when I realised something had changed in me.

It was only in 2016 when we decided to give ourselves a shot as a couple. I knew I would regret it if we didn't try, so I risked it all. I thought it would be better to regret something I had done over not knowing what it could have been and I am so very happy I did. After all, a ship is safe in harbour, but that's not what ships are for.

In 2017 he received a great job offer, an opportunity we could not refuse. He would need to move to Paris for this job but the timing of the offer could not have been better.

Both of us had been in the UK for a quite a while and longed for a change. In my opinion, London had many good aspects but I always saw it as a "passing through city". A place I loved but where I didn't really see myself forever.

I missed the sun too much, Mediterranean food, proper summers and similar cultural behaviours to that of ours. José and I always used to talk about moving closer to Portugal where his family is and where we spent many holidays and weekends away, so we didn't think twice to accept.

He said goodbye to London first and moved to Paris whilst I stayed in the UK. I didn't really want to move to Paris without a job and I had a good position in London so for about a year we had a "long" distance relationship.

Long is in quotation marks because we were really one Eurostar trip away from each other and we spend every weekend together. Every friday we would take turns and one of us would jump on the train for 3 hours and back on Sunday evening.

Eventually, in 2018 I decided to move to Paris as we got engaged and even though we were only one train away, it was (still) a train too far.

We got married in May 2019 and bought our first home shortly after deciding to start a family. We had known each other for almost 10 years, first as friends and then as a couple so there was no doubt in my mind I had the perfect partner to embark on the adventure of parenthood.

Being pregnant

On the 4th of December 2019 we got the news we were hoping for! A 'positive' symbol on six different brands of home pregnancy tests. Yes, I took 6 tests to be sure because that's how I am!

The day after I went to the lab to have a blood test done which I would need to have for my first consultation with the doctor. This would be the first of many blood works I would need to have in the following 9 months but, by far, the one that made everything real.

Later that week José and I had an appointment with an obstetrician to review the blood work but little did we know this would be the first time we would see our growing baby.

After reviewing the blood work, I was ready to go but the doctor asked me to lay on the examination table. My husband stood up silently next to me and held my hand. Neither of us were really expecting to have an ultrasound so early on but I got very excited when the doctor grabbed the gel and turned on the monitor hanging on the ceiling facing me.

We were all so quiet I think I could hear the clock ticking and marking the time as I waited for an image to appear on the screen or the doctor to say anything. It was probably a few seconds but it felt like minutes before we heard the doctor say "there it is" whilst he pointed at a little white bean on the screen.

Tears started flooding my eyes as I held José's hand and we looked at eachother. I suddenly gasped as we started to hear a sound coming through some old looking speakers. "That is the heartbeat, loud and strong," he said. I could not believe it!!!

From the home pregnancy tests, to the blood work, to the image in black and white of this little bean, to hearing the heartbeat, I was just in awe. Everytime I thought one of the above made it real we were expecting a baby, something else would happen which would make the previous seem somewhat insignificant.

When we got home, holding a little picture of our little peanut, I remembered that episode from Friends in which Rachel was not able to "see it". I laughed because I could relate now. Thankfully the doc, maybe knowing how I was, took the picture with marks around it so I could always find my baby.

At that moment, since we didn't know the sex of the baby, and because the image of that monitor remained in our memory and our hearts forever, we started calling it "caraotita". Caraota is the given name to black beans in Venezuela and it felt right to talk about our baby with a diminutive that was a bit more personal to us. Surely much more personal than peanut or bean.

From then on, between my husband and I, and to our friends and families we would say: "Caraotita is growing fast, Caraotita's heartbeat is strong, Caraotita is expected to arrive by...

Caraotita was on the way and we could not contain how happy we were. A lot of anxiety and nervousness also came with the news. First it didn't seem real, something was growing inside of me and then, there were times when we would worry about whether or not we would be good parents, but the truth is no one can ever be sure.

I think no matter how many books you read, films and documentaries you watch, or advice you listen to, you will never be sure you have what it takes to raise a child. At least we didn't.

Whilst I was in Paris, three dear friends of mine became pregnant and all of them had terrible nausea the first few months of pregnancy. One friend was still sick when she was 7 months pregnant.

The thought of it scared me for quite a while. I kept waking up thinking "today is the day my favourite food is going to make me sick". But it didn't. I thought I was lucky as I didn't get morning sickness but I got every other possible side effect. Some of which I had never even heard of as being pregnancy symptoms.

I got sudden nosebleeds, my left eye was itchy and watery every single day for the whole duration of the pregnancy, my vision also got worse and I sneezed at least 10 times per day. Everytime something new happened the doctor would say "yeah, it is normal, it is due to the pregnancy, no need to worry".

I had a runny nose but also my right nostril was blocked for the full 9 months of pregnancy and even some months post birth, bleeding gums, swollen feet, gestational diabetes and OH! How could I forget the burping! In a time where you already do not feel very sexy at all I had to add that to the   mix!

I was burping constantly and I could not do anything to stop it. As the months went by and my belly got bigger I could not handle the pressure on my bladder so every time I sneezed, I also peed a bit! I was already forgetful before getting pregnant but I got ten times worse.

As if all that was not enough, I also got a sharp pain in the right side of my stomach which worried me a lot. It happened sporadically and started towards the end of my first trimester. When I explained it to the doctor I told him I could feel as if one of my organs was detaching inside of me when I made certain movements.

I was terrified thinking that my baby was disconnecting from the placenta or my kidney was separating from something. It was very scary. Again, he said not to worry because my body was going through numerous changes and the organs were moving and making way for my baby.

This is known as growing or ligament pains which occur as the ligaments stretch to support your growing bump. Even though it is "normal", do check anything you feel with your doctor. They will be able to put your mind at ease and address anything which does require closer attention.

The worst, by far, was the sciatica pain I suffered in the first couple of months of pregnancy which I thought would only appear at the end, if at all.

If you do not know what this is I hope you never have to find out. It was an unbearable pain that started in my lower back all the way to my toes. I could not sleep or take medication for it - another perk of being pregnant! The only thing I could do, according to the doctor, was to swim as it would supposedly help ease the pain but it was winter in France and Covid-19 had already hit Europe so there was not much I could do during confinement.

Along with all of the above, I had backaches, haemorrhoids, heartburn, fatigue, constipation, sleep loss, itchy skin, gas and bloating. In summary, everything except vomiting and nausea. I swear I could not understand people who said they loved being pregnant.

If you tell me you love the idea of carrying your unborn baby, hear the first heartbeat, see the first echocardiogram or feel him or her move, then I agree but 9 months of all of those symptoms? I don't get it!

However, not all symptoms were bad, the best of them was not having my period for such a long time. It was total bliss not to have to think about buying tampons, feminine pads, mood swings and the painful menstrual cramps.

I obviously knew I wouldn't have my period for 9 months. But I wasn't aware that even after your little one is born, if you are breastfeeding your baby, your periods may not return for several months after childbirth. So in total I enjoyed a good 15 months period-free.

Another thing I didn't enjoy and was not fully aware of before being pregnant were all the changes you need to make to your diet. Everyone knows alcohol is very dangerous to the baby and therefore should be avoided completely and I was fine with that but food wise, I wasn't ready for all the things I would need to say no to.

Of course I was sure I would need to start making healthier choices like adding more vegetables and fruits to my diet, drinking more water and exercising. But I was not expecting to have to say goodbye to so many yummy things like sushi, shellfish, medium rare steaks, beef carpaccio, poached eggs, unpasteurised cheese and others. But it would all be worth it in the end.

Getting ready for the baby

We told our parents and brothers we were expecting a baby almost as soon as we found out but we waited until we had hit the end of the first trimester to tell friends and other relatives. Because my parents live in Venezuela and my brother in Edinburgh I told them via video call. I will never forget the look on my dad's face when he processed the information, he was stunned. His baby girl was going to become a mum!

We told my in-laws in person when we went to Portugal for Christmas. So I decided to buy some teddy bears wearing a baby t-shirt with a message I had printed. One for my brother- and sister-in-law (who was also pregnant at the time), and one for my mother- and father-in-law. The message for each was different but the gist of it was that they kept these teddy bears so the new baby would have something to play with when she or he came to see them.

December is itself a festive period and the news made everything so much more joyful.

When I went for my 12 weeks echocardiogram, the doctor said he could tell us the sex of the baby but due to the pandemic, my husband could not come to this appointment so I asked the doctor to write it on a piece of paper so we would find out later together.

When I arrived home, we opened the envelope but it was empty. He had just written on the inside the letter X twice. I knew right away we were expecting a girl and my husband, who is an economist, said: "Wait, how do you know?" and I said: "Well it's the chromosomes, XX is a girl and XY is a boy". He looked at me bemused and said: "but are you 100% sure?" This question made me doubt for a moment because this is not the sort of thing you want to get wrong so I went to check online and realised those biology classes back at school hadn't been for nothing. I was right!

Only then, after what seemed like forever to interpret a two letter message, we hugged and jumped for joy. At my next checkup the doctor asked if we had enjoyed his little riddle! I think my husband would have appreciated a few more letters in the message, but it was fun.

Now we knew we would have a little baby girl and that it was time to tell friends, start getting ready for her arrival and think of names.

We decided to name her Mia and we went and bought her first pair of crocheted booties. We also started to build the longest list of things we thought we would need for her. With the help from friends and family we received many of the items on the birth wish list which helped a lot and for this we are very thankful to everyone.

Many of them had already had kids so they chose to give us the stuff they considered essential and we bought everything else. Please note, don't do that! Really do some research and speak to some of your friends who are already parents. They will tell you about all the things out there which are not totally necessary to welcome your little one. You will save a ton of money and space in your house. Trust me!

When you are pregnant you are required or advised to attend a course to prepare you for the delivery of your baby. Funny they call it a course, I am sure some are good but mine lasted only 12 hours and my husband and I had to do it via video call because of the Covid-19 pandemic.

There is absolutely no way they can tell you the whole truth and nothing but the truth in that amount of time. Take into account 12 hours is less than the time it takes to deliver a baby sometimes, but that is another subject.

By now, you may have realised I never had a maternal clock telling me I had to have children. All of a sudden when I turned 35 I realised how much I wanted to be a mum.

Since I didn't have a maternal instinct in me before, I never thought of breastfeeding positively either. In fact it shocked me a bit (or a lot) whenever a friend, or worse a stranger would suddenly pop out their breast to feed their baby in front of me in a public space.

Obviously, I would never dare to say anything to a stranger nor to a friend as babies have to be fed and it is a natural thing to do. It just wasn't super natural to me to see it happening out in the open. I realise now I was the one with the problem and not them. It does not get more natural than that.

I had friends who used a nursing cover or went to a private room and I appreciated it quietly because it did not make me feel uncomfortable. But who am I to be uncomfortable? It never occurred to me to think about how they felt about it. Maybe they were secretly hoping for me to ignore it or they simply didn't care.

Since I didn't feel the urge to be a mum and I felt this way about breastfeeding, I thought if I ever had a baby I would feed them with the bottle and never breastfeed, especially not in public. After all, my mum didn't breastfeed me and I turned out alright... I think...

It was only after I got pregnant and heard my baby girl's heartbeat for the first time when I knew I wanted to breastfeed her, not only because it would be very beneficial for both of us, but also because I wanted to feel that connection with her everyone talked about. It would be the one thing I could give her that only I could do and no one else.

Throughout the duration of my pregnancy, José and I bought books, spoke to friends and family, read magazines from the doctor's office and searched online to be as prepared as we could be to welcome Mia.

But as you are bringing a little human being into this world, no amount of research will ever get you close to being ready for the biggest change and the most important role in your life. You can start to prepare but, the truth is, you prepare, practice and learn as you go, every day. And it never stops.

A few years back I had a breast augmentation surgery in Venezuela which is a pretty common thing to do there. When I was growing up I didn't really feel at all comfortable with my breasts size so as soon as I turned 20 I decided to have this surgery to improve my self esteem and feel more confident in my own skin.

I got silicone implants of 200 cc and went from a size 32A to 34B and I felt so much better wearing a bikini afterwards. Sure, I could have gone bigger, but I just wanted to feel great about myself and not for my breasts to enter through a door before my nose did. There is absolutely nothing wrong with that but it was not what I needed.

Nevertheless, when I was pregnant one of my worries was not being able to breastfeed because I was afraid I wouldn't be able to produce milk but my obstetrician (OB) assured me there wouldn't be any issues with milk supply and he was right. Imagine someone who never in her life had thought of breastfeeding, now was worried about not being able to do so! How ironic!

Let's go back to the "course" my husband and I took to prepare for Mia's arrival. Please don't get me wrong if I sound unappreciative about it, it is only my personal experience. However, I definitely recommend taking some kind of course because in the worst case scenario you will learn something. I reiterate that this is not a campaign to put you off breastfeeding or paying for courses to prepare you.

Now, imagine for a second how this course worked for us. Let me remind you: my husband is Portuguese and I am from Venezuela; we met in London, got married in Portugal and now live in France... I get lost sometimes too and someday maybe I will even expand on this in another book!

Oh right! I forgot to mention: we are not fluent in French! However, we do speak enough French to get by day to day and we understand more than we speak.

When we signed up for the course we knew it would have to be online due to the pandemic. Now, if you are trying to speak another language other than your mother tongue, then you will know how hard it is to understand someone over the phone. I mean, it's already hard to understand them in person!

We tried to find someone in the Hospital who could dictate the course for us in English, Spanish or Portuguese, as we are fluent in those languages, but we did not succeed. It would have to be in French and with a lot of use of Google translate. (I was not paid to name them, this is a free ad!).

During the course we quickly understood in France most of the staff in the Hospital where Mia was to be born were pro-breastfeeding. But not only that, they were completely against bottle-feeding, and I am not talking just about formula, that was a big No No!!! They were also against feeding a baby expressed milk.

Once, in one of the lessons, I told the midwife I would like to extract milk so my husband could also feed Mia from time to time, or help me during the night, and she was not at all happy about that. She said there was no need, I solely had that responsibility and he could help and connect with the baby by other means such as changing the diaper, rocking her to sleep, etc. I was shocked!

She also said if you bottle-feed babies, regardless if it has formula or breastmilk, they become lazy and reject the breast afterwards because they have to work more and it is easier to drink from the bottle. This was not true for us as I will explain later.

After this video call, my husband and I discussed the matter, and decided to put this advice on hold and to trust our own instincts when the time came. I thought maybe it was just this one person who felt like this and we were "unlucky" enough to have her assigned to do our whole course as she was the one who understood a little English, and could answer any questions that we couldn't pose in French. Little did I know all of the nurses in the hospital felt this way too.

During the course, they drilled into my head nothing is more nourishing than breastmilk and nothing more powerful than colostrum. They might be right, but I feel that they need to get better at explaining this. For many women it is just unbearable to breastfeed or they just simply do not produce milk or colostrum the same way others do.

There are many reasons why some women can have a low milk supply, such as a history of Polycystic Ovarian Syndrome, Diabetes, Thyroid or other hormonal disorders. There is also a rare medical condition called mammary Hypoplasia, in which there isn't enough milk-producing glandular tissue within the breast. It might be rare but it exists.

If you, God forbid, were to suffer from any of these or simply could not take the pain of a hungry baby sucking at your breasts to get whatever drop you have, you would immediately feel like a failure and the consequences of this happening could be very dangerous.

I feel the need, from time to time, or paragraph to paragraph, to apologise and remind you I am in no way on a mission to attack health staff, midwives, doctors, mums, friends, etc, etc. I am just trying to tell you about what I lived through so that you can relate if anything I am saying happens to you during your pregnancy or delivery of your precious baby.

During our preparatory course, we had 2 hours devoted to breastfeeding, one for theory and the other for practice. Remember, we did this via videoconference so the theory was "fine", but the practice part? I mean the whole thing is laughable.

I put "fine" in quotation marks because the one hour dedicated to theory on breastfeeding was not at all even an introduction to what nursing actually is. It isn't a secret that many women struggle with the initiation of breastfeeding. Therefore, the purpose of these courses should be to really dig into the depths of knowledge mothers should have in order to be as ready as they can for when the time comes.

Instead, the hour was spent talking about colostrum, advantages of breastfeeding against giving formula, the connection between mother and baby and the way the milk is produced and how the position of the baby's tongue is key for them to feed properly. This is all well and good but when the baby is stuck to your breasts, they hurt, and you can't see how his or her tongue is positioned, you simply cannot think about the advantages of breastfeeding due to the pain.

The hour of the course dedicated to breastfeeding practice consisted of the midwife sitting two metres away from the camera holding a doll and showing us the different positions in which you can nurse. Then she showed us some of the devices which could help "alleviate discomfort", as they call it, such as nipple shields, nursing pillows, nipple cream, etc.

I should have known then that if there are so many things out there designed to relieve the pain it is because the whole thing is not a walk in the park. But the truth is, I didn't know it was going to hurt that much.

Whilst I was pregnant, only one of my former colleagues from University was extremely open and honest about how much breastfeeding hurt. She had just had her second child and she posted on social media photos of her nipples completely destroyed. They had cracks deeper than the Grand Canyon, but I thought to myself maybe she was not producing milk and that the baby was desperate to feed.

I asked her about it and I thank God that she was so open, because I didn't know it then, but later I would be very grateful to know I wasn't alone. She said with her first child she didn't even try much and gave up quickly since her breast would bleed so much.

She said once she noticed her first child had blood in her mouth and she was stunned thinking it was coming from her baby's mouth. It wasn't until she looked at her own breast that she saw how she was bleeding. This is when I got really scared.

You could say maybe this conversation played in my head and somehow predisposed me to having issues breastfeeding because of how shocked I was. But I completely disagree. I have had this conversation with two friends since having Mia and they have not experienced any excruciating pain or injuries on their nipples. In fact they quite enjoyed it from the very first moment they breastfed.

Although it was shocking, I do appreciate her being so honest about it because if she hadn't I would have definitely felt as a failure later on. Whereas after breastfeeding Mia, I would have someone to turn to, who, I knew, would understand.

Meeting Mia for the first time

A month or so after this conversation, I delivered Mia via an emergency C-Section. She didn't turn in the womb so she was in breech position. In simple terms she was bum down instead of head down. We knew early on that most likely we wouldn't be able to have her by natural birth. My C-Section was scheduled for Friday 7th of August 2020 at 10:00am but she was in a bit of a hurry and could not wait to come into the world.

The previous evening, we were at home. We normally have dinner around 8:00pm but because I wouldn't be able to eat anything in the morning before my surgery, we decided to have a late dinner. Also, we wanted to make time because we would leave our dog with a friend who would take care of him during the time we would be at the hospital and we wanted to take him as late as possible.

I was sitting on the couch, removing my nail polish and going through the checklist of things you need to do before being admitted to hospital. Next step would be to have a shower with Betadine. Very Carrie-like. Stephen King would have loved my performance - but I never got round to it! (Next time I will make him proud!)

My water broke at 7:23pm!

I would say that under stressful situations I can remain more calm than my husband but when my water broke I panicked. I thought Mia would be making her appearance as I ran to the bathroom.

During the famous "preparation course" they tell you if your water breaks there is no need to hurry to the hospital. They ask you to call, to time your contractions and to check how dilated your cervix is. When you call your practitioner or the hospital, they should ask you a few questions and guide you through it as the timing is different for almost every mum-to-be.

However, if you have a breech baby, like Mia, you'll likely go to the hospital as soon as you're in active labour, especially if you have complications like Gestational Diabetes or Preeclampsia, which need monitoring sooner rather than later.

I was very surprised to find out how calm my husband was. He called the hospital and told them what had happened and then, very much at ease he came and said to me: "Let's go to the hospital everything is going to be ok." Thank God I'd listened to the part of the course where they tell you to prepare your bags very early on.

Mine were already packed two weeks before the due date but they would have been ready anyway because the C-section was planned for the day after. Babies can come well before their due date and when you least expect it so make sure you have them ready!

He picked up the bags, Mia's carrier and our dog's stuff and arranged them at the door. We called our friend who was going to look after our dog and told her we were on our way to drop him off early.

Whilst all of this was happening I could still feel a trickle of water and I had a huge diaper on. I couldn't stop crying so I called my mum when we were in the car and she managed to calm me down a bit.

However, I couldn't stop thinking Mia was going to be left without any water in her little tight pool and I realised then how you forget absolutely everything you learned in the course about how this works. Some women's waters break and they don't give birth until the next day but you don't think about that when you are the one going through it.

The other fear I had was arriving at the hospital and being so dilated they would make me have a natural birth even though Mia was not in the correct birthing position.

When we arrived, the hospital car park was closed and we could not find a way in. Can you believe it? We weren't allowed in through the 'Emergency' entrance either. It certainly felt like an emergency!

Then a nurse told us to go around the back where there was a phone to call-in for someone to come get us. But when we got there and dialled in no one picked up the phone. Neither were there any parking spaces outside which were walking distance to the hospital. José said he would go and investigate, as he left, he told me he would be back as soon as he could and he loved me. Oh, and not to panic. Easy.

So there I was, sitting alone in the entrance of a Hospital car park, wearing a very wet adult diaper, in pre-labour at nine in the evening and my husband, god love him, runs over with sweat on his brow saying he's found where we need to go so I can deliver our little girl.

We finally arrived at the maternity unit where they started monitoring me and Mia. I was panicking thinking they would make me have a natural birth given she was not in the right position. However, as I was only 4 cm dilated, had no contractions, and because we hadn't had dinner in the evening, they were able to do the C-Section that night which was extremely quick.

Even though I didn't get my obstetrician to do the surgery as my baby came one day before the arranged C-Section, the team who treated me and Mia during the birth were the best. I remember in particular the anesthesiologist who was so, so sweet to us.

Unfortunately, due to the pandemic my mum was in Venezuela and could not be with me whilst I had Mia.

However, the anesthesiologist had a calming and attentive nature that overwhelmed me. She knew how to take my mind off my worries, distract me and help me focus on what was going on. She explained everything as it was happening and gave me the epidural. I remember being very scared by this since people had told me it would hurt a lot and I was surprised when she said it was done.

I felt everything she said I was going to feel but with no pain whatsoever. She talked to us continuously, describing everything she was seeing and what the surgeon was doing. She even asked for my husband's phone and became our photographer as she took the first ever pictures of us as a family of three.

By 10:51pm we were the parents of a beautiful, healthy baby girl and we could not be happier than at that very moment.

Mia was finally here, after nine months of waiting. From my dreams to the black and white ultrasounds, I was finally seeing her face to face for the first time. No matter which words I try to use to explain the emotion I felt in that moment, none of them go near describing the feeling of pure joy, unconditional love, the world just fell from beneath me, for in that moment only she and I existed in the world.

Suddenly tears started running down my cheeks. I could not understand how we could have made her. How is it possible we had now created this little human being when we had spent months looking at mobile apps where her size was compared to that of beans, peanuts, lemons, avocados, etc. I knew then I had become someone else and I would prioritise her over myself a zillion times over.

Whilst they did the checks on Mia and gave me my stitches they put her skin to skin on José's chest and I could see them nearby. He was so afraid he could break her as she was so tiny and fragile but it was just beautiful to see them together, she looked so comfortable and peaceful whilst he was just in awe of her.

I can't really explain what I felt then because so many emotions were happening at the same time but pure happiness doesn't even begin to cover it. I am sure she felt protected and comfortable, as did I, because I knew in that very instant I could not have chosen a better person to be the father of my daughter and my companion through this journey.

I didn't know then if it was the anaesthesia or simply my emotions but I felt very little pain from the C-section. A couple of hours later I was able to get up, walk around, go to the bathroom and sit down without the need of any help.

Don't get me wrong, I felt some discomfort but I had been expecting excruciating pain since C-section surgery is very invasive but perhaps it is because I expected it to be so painful that it actually wasn't at all.

If you don't already know, you will continue to bleed considerably for a few days after the birth. To help with this you can find hundreds of postpartum control briefs on the market which are essentially like adult diapers for incontinence. They are available in supermarkets, pharmacies and online.

Most are disposable and come with different designs to make them "pretty". On the diaper pack, it is claimed they help you stay comfortable, dry, and more confident but to be honest, I wouldn't recommend them, especially in the case of a C-section.

I had bought a pack of these diapers but they were only useful to me when my water broke. After my C-section, the high-fitting waistband would snag on the stitches from the scar and it was very painful. I also didn't enjoy the feeling of wearing a diaper, but it all comes down to personal preferences.

After trying them for one day I followed the advice of a friend which was to buy cotton panties and the thickest menstrual pads available. This way I felt more comfortable and a lot more like myself.

I personally recommend you do the same because not only will you be able to choose a more comfortable fabric in a wide range of colours, but you will also be able to use these low rise briefs in the future when your bloody days are over. No pun intended!

Breastfeeding

Later, when we were in the recovery room the games began. I say games because the nurse came by to "help me feed Mia" but all she did was put her on my chest and ask me to point my nipple to her nose so she would open her mouth and latch on, which she did but it hurt a lot.

Of course Mia wasn't doing it properly but I didn't know that then and the nurse didn't stay long enough to see and help us through it.

It was at this very moment I remembered the conversation with my friend I mentioned before, and thought to myself: "maybe this is how it goes and it won't hurt like this after a few tries".

If I remembered anything at this point about the course was that babies need to latch correctly to increase milk production and feed properly. Unfortunately, all I could feel was my nipples getting sore as she was just sucking the tip of them.

Nurses would come into our room every other hour to check on my baby and ask whether she had fed or not. We were in the hospital for 3 days and Mia was on my breast for what seems now like every other 20 minutes.

Once, one of the nurses said to me: "Look, she is hungry, she's putting her fist in her mouth, it is a sign she is starving, you need to feed her" Mia had literally fallen asleep after sucking for 10 minutes before the nurse came in. I did put her on again and not once did anyone tell me her mouth was not positioned correctly but I knew something was wrong.

Whilst I had many friends who struggled with breastfeeding, as I said before, I had others for whom it was the easiest thing in the world and they even refer to it as a relief.

Having a child is a huge change for you and your partner, and if on top of that you add the stress of not being able to feed your own baby, then it is pretty uphill from there.

I have a friend who had been given formula in the hospital since her breasts were so sore. But that was never an option for me. They just kept pushing for me to breastfeed and whilst I really wanted to I was about to drop the whole thing all together.

One of the nurses, who was very nice to us throughout our stay in the hospital, told me to use the nipple shields we had with us to alleviate discomfort. However, my breasts were already too sore to feel much relief but they did help a bit. I find it ironic now that most healthcare staff there were against bottle feeding but they would recommend the use of nipple shields which to me look pretty much like the teat of a baby bottle.

By the third day I could not wait to be discharged from hospital and was very happy to go home and return to our own environment. I thought without the pressure we could find solutions ourselves given the hospital did not.

When we got home something happened which had not happened in the hospital. I cried from the pain Mia was causing me. Whilst she was sucking, or attempting to, I said to my husband in despair: "I can't do this!" I had been wanting to cry for so long but I was scared to cry in the hospital in case they thought I was suffering from Postpartum Depression.

I was made whole when Mia was born and there was no doubt in my mind that I was happy but the pain I felt breastfeeding her was too much for me. However, Postpartum Depression is very common and it is important for you to be able to identify it early. There is no reason to be ashamed. So, if you happen to realise you are having feelings of extreme sadness, indifference or anxiety, do seek professional help or talk to someone you trust and you feel comfortable with to address it early.

Going back to our first day back home with Mia, as soon as I started crying my husband, on the other hand, feeling anything but useless, said: "I wish I could do it for you or help you in some way but I don't know what to do. Let's make her a bottle and think things through" It was a conundrum because it felt like a huge relief but at the same time I felt like I had failed.

We did make her a bottle and whilst I was giving it to her, tears kept running down my cheeks because I wished I could be feeding her with my breast. I think it was the first time she actually felt full since she didn't show signs of hunger until about 2 to 3 hours later. Whilst she slept I used the time to have a long warm shower and put cream on my nipples which were so sore, cracked and bleeding.

Later that night, we called our sister-in-law who had had a baby 6 months earlier. We were very open in terms of the questions we asked, which we hadn't done before, not to her. To my surprise, she had struggled with breastfeeding as well, but she had kept at it and succeeded.

She lives in Portugal and because of the pandemic we were not able to be with them when their daughter was born so, I never saw her in the first few days breastfeeding my niece. When I saw her breastfeeding her baby on a rocking chair from afar and through a video call, she looked very peaceful and not like a person who was in pain.

Without knowing it, I was longing for support and understanding and I decided to be open about the issue I was having. So, one by one, I spoke to all my friends who had become mums for the first time recently.

I talked to another friend who said a few magic words: "I couldn't do it either and I don't feel less of a mum because of it. Stop beating yourself up about it and do what feels right. If you are happy, Mia will be too! I made my own connection by looking into my daughter's eyes whilst I gave her the bottle". I needed to hear this and know it would be ok if I could not manage to breastfeed her due to the pain I was experiencing.

Not being able to breastfeed properly can be frustrating and distressing for you, your partner and your baby. If your baby has a poor breastfeeding latch you can not only have sore nipples but your baby will not be able to drain your breast which then will lead to reduced milk supply, poor weight gain, and put you at increased risk of blocked milk ducts and/or Mastitis.

Mastitis! That is another word I remembered from the so-called "course" and one of which I was very much afraid of as I had heard the pain is worse than what you get from sore nipples. So that afternoon I chose the lesser of two evils.

My breasts were huge because Mia had not breastfed for a while so I decided to try extracting milk using a breast pump. I thought that way I could decide the amount of suction I was willing to suffer and get some comfort. It would also help me to continue producing milk because I wanted to give breastfeeding another try.

Then, my husband and I scheduled a consultation for the next morning with an independent midwife and lactation consultant who had a practice right on our doorstep. In the meantime, throughout the day I continued extracting milk and applying Lanolin cream whilst I bottle fed Mia with just formula. The difference in her was astronomical, she was sleeping much better and the time between feedings gradually increased.

Seeing the light at the end of the tunnel

The appointment with the lactation consultant was everything I wish had happened in the hospital or during the course. Her name was Elsie, and I loved how she was neither judgemental nor opinionated. Elsie was like that friend who said to me "whatever you decide to do is ok".

The first thing I did when we sat down was start crying and I swore to her I didn't have Postpartum Depression. Elsie got the joke and smiled. She asked us why we were there and what we wanted to achieve.

With tears running through my cheeks I tried to explain why I was crying and Elsie said: "If you want to keep trying to breastfeed I can help you but if you want to stop I can also give you a prescription to help you stop producing milk" Music to my ears. Finally someone was interested in what I wanted and not what they felt was right.

We said we wanted to keep trying but she was very surprised to see the size of my breasts and could not understand how they let me out of the hospital like this. Elsie was shocked to see the cracks on my nipples and how hard my breasts were. She said I came really close to having Mastitis and I think I could feel that too.

She said I could continue extracting milk during the day and only breastfeed Mia three times a day for the next 2 days to help my nipples recover. In order to aid the nipples heal faster she recommended I gently apply freshly extracted breast milk. Apparently this is the best thing there is but I knew this already and had tried it at home but it didn't give me as much relief as applying the Lanolin ointment.

Besides continuing to apply the cream and breast milk Elsie also advised using warm compresses and an occasional salt water rinse.

However, the one thing which gave me the most relief, also advised by her, was to try as much as possible to leave my breasts uncovered. The bra and nursing pads hurt me terribly because every time my nipples started to dry they would stick to the material. Imagine cutting your knee and having tight jeans that are always chafing the wound. Then imagine the fabric stuck to the dried wound... You get the idea...

If you already know something about breastfeeding you will be aware your breasts will be leaking milk constantly. If you didn't, well, you just found out! That's why there are so many types of nursing pads on the market. I asked Elsie what I was going to do about this leaking breast milk. She said I could use milk collection cups to save the milk secreted naturally without having to suffer the discomfort of the milk pump and in doing so it would also help the wounds heal.

Very early on, I had bought these little milk collection cups and I am glad I did. After listening to her advice, whilst sitting on my couch shirtless I would put them on to save as much as I could of that precious and valuable liquid.

Every drop counted! Speaking so freely about this to a close friend is one thing, but to someone I didn't know? Readers might think I am comparing this to milking cows, but I don't care and you shouldn't either.

So, in the first 5 minutes I realised this woman was without a doubt going to be a huge help and I would be in her debt forever. More importantly, she showed me some other tricks like how to position Mia so she would latch on correctly.

1. <u>Positioning is more important than it seems</u>

Elsie asked me to show her how I fed Mia and to do so exactly as I would do at home. I sat down and held Mia in the Cradle position. This, she said, is the easiest way to nurse and is the best method for feeding older or more experienced babies.

It is definitely the most popular method and in fact, was the technique recommended to me during the preparation course and whilst I was in hospital. However, with this method, Mia could not achieve a correct latch and my nipples hurt horribly. I was as stiff as a rock, very tense anticipating the pain I was about to feel. Elsie said I was holding Mia correctly but my posture was completely wrong.

She pointed out how much I was hunching over and that I needed to relax so my baby would feel that too. However, I could not find a way to relax because I knew how painful it would be.

The Cradle Hold looks like the following. Trust me, you will be smiling too while nursing your baby if you do it correctly.

But then Elsie showed me another position which would change my whole perspective of breastfeeding, and

Mia's too. This position is called the Cross-Cradle Hold which is similar to the Cradle but is better for newborn babies who are still learning how to latch properly or for babies who have difficulty feeding.

I remembered trying the Cross-Cradle Hold once in hospital, after a web search, but it hurt a lot then. Being with Elsie I realised I must have been doing something wrong before. Because this time, following Elsie's precise instructions, Mia's latch was spot on and even with my sore nipples, it didn't hurt as much as it did when I had tried it before.

This hold is similar to the cradle one, but your arms are positioned slightly differently. Instead of supporting your baby's head in the crook of your arm, you use the hand of that arm to support your breast while your opposite arm comes around the back of your baby.

There are, in fact, multiple positions you can use to nurse your baby and I encourage you to try them all since in this respect there is no rule of thumb. You might find one that is better for you, but for me this was the best, at least in the beginning. Afterwards, you might be able to pick and choose what to do according to where you are and how you feel.

2.   Practical Pacifier Replacement:

Elsie looked on while I fed Mia to see if there were any other aspects which could be improved. She did notice my baby was a 'desperate eater'. Mia was so hungry she always sucked with extreme force but because my breast had not been properly stimulated by her, the flow of milk was less than what it should have been. It was here when Elsie gave me the next tip that would change my perspective about breastfeeding.

The technique, known as a practical pacifier substitute, consists of using your pinky finger to soothe your baby before breastfeeding. I thought this was great as it is free and always available.

Elsie asked me to clean my hands and insert the tip of my pinky finger into Mia's mouth. To do so, I simply needed to lay Mia on the side I wished to breastfeed, and turn the opposite free hand palm-side up to let her suck on the tip of my finger for a bit, whilst allowing it to rest gently on the roof of her mouth.

Elsie had noticed Mia's first sucks were the most aggressive so she told me to feel when the sucking on my pinky finger was more moderate. I could totally feel how the first few sucks were very strong but soon enough they became more subtle. Elsie asked me to do this every time I was getting ready to breastfeed to understand when to remove my finger and replace it with my breast.

I wouldn't have to do this forever, she said, but long enough until Mia understood what type of sucking pattern to make and when I recognised the best moment to replace the finger with my breast. If she was more relaxed, her sucking rhythm would change from being fast with just a few drops of milk let-down, to being slow with a higher flow.

This made a huge difference then, because even with cracked nipples it hurt less and I could understand when to put her in position going forward. I did this for about the first three weeks and after that I didn't need to, it was like riding a bike.

3.   Correct latch

Any lactation consultant will tell you getting the latch right is the most important aspect of successful nursing; and they are right. This is key for your baby to extract milk efficiently and for you to feel little to no discomfort. This last part almost makes me laugh! I couldn't have imagined there would never be discomfort whilst nursing, but I was wrong.

There are many ways to make sure your baby is latched on correctly, but here is some useful advice you will see in pretty much any respective website:

- Always support your baby with pillows so you aren't hunching over.

- With one breast in one hand and the baby's back supported in the other one, bring your baby (not just the head, but the whole body) close enough so they can easily reach your nipple.

- Tickle their upper lip with your nipple until they open their mouth wide.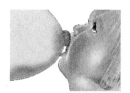

- Next, bring your baby towards the nipple and not the other way around, which is one of the things I was doing wrong.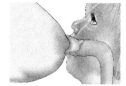

- Remember your baby's chin should touch the breast first and they should latch onto more breast tissue under the nipple than above it.

- Your baby's lips should be fully flanged like fish lips and should wrap around your areola.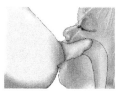

- Last but not least, make sure nothing is blocking your baby's nose. Like your breast skin above the nipple or clothes etc.

If by any chance you have trouble breastfeeding your baby, do have your newborn's latch checked, ideally by a healthcare professional trained in breastfeeding support, or by a qualified lactation consultant or breastfeeding specialist. An expert will be able to determine whether your baby has a tongue-tie or any other condition that could make the latch-on process more difficult.

4.   <u>Get comfortable whilst breastfeeding</u>

One of the mistakes I made when I first started nursing Mia was that since the very first day at the hospital I was always moving my body towards her as I thought this was the way to make sure she achieved a good latch. However, this meant I had a bad posture and when pain started I got more and more tense.

When Elsie asked me to breastfeed Mia she could see my whole posture was wrong. As I mentioned previously, I was very tense and my back was curved, in part anticipating the pain, I guess, and trying to maintain an uncomfortable position for a prolonged period of time can lead to significant back, shoulder, and neck pain so I really needed to change this.

If you are pregnant now for the first time, maybe you can't imagine how long you are going to be nursing your baby. But trust me it will be for a long time and this applies to formula too, not just breastfeeding.

If you feed your baby in an unsupported sitting position, it will get uncomfortable pretty quickly and the constant shifts in positioning to try to feel better will disrupt your baby's breastfeeding and can result in irritability and increased hunger.

I really recommend sitting in a reclined position with your baby lying in your arms in the Cross-Cradle position I spoke of before. But whichever position you decide to use, make sure you are comfortable and well supported with pillows under your arms and behind your back.

In time, you will find the best position for you and you will be able to mix it up once you get the hang of it. When Mia was 1 month old I could already feed her laying down with her next to me and in every other nursing position without any pain whatsoever.

5. Relax

You know the saying "dogs can sense your fear"? Hang on before you crucify me for what seems like I am comparing babies to dogs, I just want to say there is another one that says if you are relaxed your baby will be too. This is not just a saying, it is so so true!

Elsie said she could see I wasn't relaxed and I obviously wasn't. I was in fear of the pain. I was scared to resent Mia in some way for the pain she was causing me, so, whilst being comfortable, having a good latch, an appropriate nursing position and anticipating your baby's cues are important, being relaxed has a weight of its own.

You do have to try your best to relax by listening to a playlist, visualising your happy place, take a few slow, deep breaths and opt for a change of environment if it is too stressful where you are. Many people say, and I do believe it now, that a baby can sense if you're tense and nervous about breastfeeding. If you are, nothing is going to go well in that nursing session since he or she won't latch on correctly.

Talking about all of this reminds me of my mum when she talks about sushi. Don't worry I will explain why. She hates sushi, but more than that, she does not understand how anyone likes it as many people, including myself, said to her: "you have to try it a few times before you love it". Her answer to this was always: "why do I have to put myself through something horrible a few times to end up loving it? I either like it or I don't, period. I will not force myself to eat it".

I saw nursing a bit like this... an effort you make selflessly. You think you are making it for a tiny human being who came out of you and you put yourself through the pain just because people say breastmilk is the best for them, but in the end, if done correctly, you will end up loving it.

Again, breastfeeding for me was a challenge, one I wanted to succeed at, but it isn't an issue for everyone.

More importantly, if it ends up not working for you, **DO NOT** beat yourself up over it. As I said before, you can have a few moments which are both your own and no one else's and it doesn't matter if you are giving your baby formula, breast milk through a bottle or breastfeeding. What matters is that you and your baby are happy.

After leaving Elsie's office my whole life as a mum changed and I will be forever grateful to her. I had a positive outlook towards the future but more importantly I knew I was not the only one with issues and it would be ok if none of the advice she gave us worked.

One of the key things I understood was that I needed to find out what made me happy so Mia would be too. A couple of days later, my husband and I discovered what worked for us which is not necessarily the advice given by many midwives.

We found out Mia slept a lot better after drinking formula at night than with breastmilk. I am no scientist but there are hundreds, if not thousands of studies which certify that breastfed babies tend to wake from sleep more easily and sleep for shorter periods of time. Whereas, nearly all babies who sleep through the night by the age of 3 months are formula-fed.

Time for a quick repeat! I am not advising you to do this, this is simply what worked for me and it is important to know the alternatives available for you, your baby and your partner.

Since breast milk is easier to digest, it can contribute to more frequent night wakings. Formula, on the other hand, is harder to digest and may help your baby sleep a little longer.

So, whilst I was trying to heal my nipples, and because I didn't have a huge bank of breast milk to give her through the night, we gave her formula. Using the milk pump was still hurtful at times and I wasn't quite clear how many ounces (or millilitres) of expressed milk I would need to have to make sure she was satisfied. So with formula, Mia's dad could also help out by feeding her throughout the night and I could get a bit more sleep. Happy wife, happy life!

It is known that babies who do 'mixed' feeding, also known as 'combined' feeding, can sometimes reject the breast because they have to make less of an effort with the bottle and they can get lazy.

If you end up thinking of starting mixed feeding, make sure you know what the experts say, and do some research on how to do it and when.

There are many articles out there and your lactation consultant should be able to answer some of your questions. It is very important you know how it can affect your baby and what it could do to your own milk supply since you'll be breastfeeding less frequently.

Additionally, if and when you do decide to transition to bottle feeding, regardless if it is breastmilk or formula, bear in mind there will be a lot of washing and sterilising to do. Breastfeeding is cheap and in a way easier as it is already prepped and you don't have to heat it or wash a ton of baby bottles after. It is always available and I loved how convenient it was in that sense.

If you do end up introducing bottle feeding, make sure you add to your baby wish list a great bottle warmer. I really recommend investing some money on this. A friend had told me to get one from Beaba Bib Expresso which warmed the milk in 1 minute but was quite expensive. However, I didn't give it much thought and got one in the mid-price range that heated the bottle in 5 minutes.

A difference of 4 minutes didn't sound like much to me back when I was pregnant but trust me, it is a very long time when you add to that a baby crying desperately to be fed.

I do not have the necessary training to tell you exactly what to do but I can tell you what worked for us. As I mentioned before, during the night Mia had formula exclusively using the slowest flow teat and throughout the day she was breastfed on demand and thankfully she never rejected the breast or showed signs of frustration.

I have a friend who did the same as me and her baby would not take the bottle from her, but she would from her partner or someone else in the family. Little by little she started to understand which feeds were with the bottle and finally she ended up taking it from her mum too. Babies are much more intelligent than we give them credit for.

Again, find out what works for you and disregard what everyone else thinks. As long as your baby is growing, gaining weight and happy, little matters what others say. It is no one else's business to judge whether you breastfeed your baby or give him or her formula. You are still a mum and a hell of a good one!

Whilst I was trying to find a way to breastfeed Mia in which we were both happy, I started thinking about the first 2 weeks with her and I realised how little preparation and support I had from the hospital, the course, and even people who had become mums. There is a lot people do not talk about and it is super important we start being open about these subjects.

I started asking friends about their experiences and telling them about mine. I was surprised to hear how many of them had received guidance that was perceived as uncaring, unsupportive, or harmful at times. But I wish I had known this before because I would have been able to identify it.

There is a lot of talk out there about violent births, obstetric abuse in childbirth, honouring and respecting birth plans, etc. but there is not enough talk about how many women struggle with breastfeeding and are looked down upon by health practitioners and society when and if they give up.

Sure, you could say I picked the wrong preparation course or I was unlucky and I really, really do hope that is the case, but after speaking to many friends who had babies around the same time as I did, and in different countries, the story didn't seem all that different.

The truth is that, for my husband and I, preparation occurred once we stepped foot into our home with our baby. It is only then, when you have your baby in your arms and there is no health staff around you, that you start to realise how unprepared you actually are.

So, I need to emphasise that care and support from clinicians during breastfeeding initiation is much more important than whether or not you get to learn about breastfeeding the hard way and the innumerable ways you can position your baby. Therefore, if you are pregnant now, make sure you choose a course which has very good reviews, if possible from people you know, talk to friends, ask uncomfortable questions, break the taboo.

It can be that you have no issues at all, and I really pray that is the case. I have many friends who didn't suffer at all when breastfeeding but sadly they are not the majority. So the minute you feel something isn't right, go and see a lactation professional or try some of the tricks I outlined here.

More importantly, if it ends up not working for you, do not beat yourself up. Many people talk about how the connection with your baby is directly related to breastfeeding. They are wrong.

Your baby is part of you and when he or she left their little pool to come into the world, they were still attached through a cord. It doesn't get more connected than that, but if you adopted or had a baby through surrogacy your baby is not less yours than Mia is mine.

Whilst I really wanted to breastfeed Mia, and I ended up enjoying it, I felt connected to her when I gave her the bottle too. As long as your baby is close to you and you are looking into each other's eyes you become one.

Life changes for more than the baby and the mum

Speaking of breaking taboos, I can't finish this book without recognising our partners. Almost always when there is a birth, people ask how the mum and the baby are and I can see why. But even a few months after, they are still so concerned about the baby and mum, that they tend to leave the dad or partner out of the equation. However, it is important to understand that having a baby changes not only your life.

I mentioned before that whilst I was struggling with breastfeeding my husband felt powerless. If you knew him you would quickly realise he likes to help and he does soooo much to make me happy but during this time he could not and I could see how it affected him.

There is a lot of talk about Postpartum Depression in women but hardly anyone stops to think about how the dad is coping with all of the changes. During the prep course, which dads or partners are advised to attend, I felt they are just regarded as an add on, someone who is supposed to be there but matters little to the delivery and aftercare of the baby.

Partners are advised to rub the woman's back, help her relax, help her breathe, rock or burp the baby, etc. but who helps them?

When we got back from the hospital I could see my husband wanted to do more but felt like there was nothing he could do. Family and friends would text or call to ask about Mia and me but who asked him how he felt?

If someone did, he would obviously say he was happy but he felt his hands were tied and couldn't do more than cook or wash the dishes and only be there to help me and Mia.

I remember it used to bother him, and me too, that in the prep course, and some of the books we bought, they used the terms "mum" "baby" and "caregiver". Father was hardly ever used. It seemed he was just there to be a 'plus one'.

Although I have his agreement to talk about this, he is very private when it comes to personal stuff. So, when I saw he was frustrated we talked about it but I could hardly do more than try to help or give him some advice. I thought he should speak to someone who could relate more and listen without judgement.

I asked him to talk to his friends but he wouldn't as he thought he was the only one who felt like this and that it wasn't a big deal. Until one day we were on a video call with some friends and he brought up the subject with a guy who had recently become a dad too. He went on and on about how he felt when he brought his daughter home and the two of them had a very honest and open conversation that really changed everything. He knew it was ok to feel like this and more importantly, he could feed Mia and do more than just burp and change her nappies.

I am telling you this because although it was not serious, Postpartum Depression in men is real and it can happen silently so you really need to put yourself in their shoes as it is not just your world that suddenly changed.

According to research published in the Journal of the American Medical Association, about 10% of fathers become depressed before or just after their baby is born.

So baby blues is not just a thing that can happen to mothers, and I sincerely hope you can tell the difference between your partner feeling tired from lack of sleep and feeling glum, so you can talk about it and help him.

I think I have covered more than what I wanted to speak of when I decided to write this book but I hope this tool gives you some courage and advice if you ever need it to understand we are not born knowing everything and that even when we try, there is always more you can learn.

We continue to learn everyday as parents and now we have the most perfect 19 month old baby girl. Every parent would say this about their children but believe me: We do have the best baby ever! She is smart, playful, happy and cheerful, loves animals, eats everything (very well on her own now) and sleeps almost 12 hours straight throughout the night.

Sure, I have a scar on my stomach now that I see every time I look in the mirror but it reminds me of the miracle we created and whilst there were some difficult moments, they remained as that, just moments that didn't last for long and went away quickly.

Every day I am thankful to have the honour of having her call me mum, and the sight of her smile erases any worry I might have about whether I am enough for her or worthy of her. As long as I am doing my very best and she is happy I know I am doing it right.

Mia really is the best thing that ever happened to us and whilst she is growing very fast, I will always remember her as this tiny little human being who showed me what unconditional love really is.

Thinking back to those first few days at home with Mia, they were without a shadow of a doubt a challenge. But one I would do over and over again because the real challenge is not what we put our attention towards, sometimes the real challenge comes from within.

All I want you to appreciate from reading through my experience becoming a first time mum is that, no matter what you do, people will always judge and find reasons to make a comment they think they are entitled to make. Just make sure **YOU** are happy, relaxed and enjoying every bit of being a mum.

There definitely will be ups and downs, but rest assured you have the power within you to pull through anything. You are a super mum!

Remember, it is your baby, your breasts and all you can do is your best.

Summary of golden tips

I have outlined below the golden tips Elsie gave me for breastfeeding so you can refer to them easily. I hope you never need them and you are like those friends of mine who did not suffer at all breastfeeding their babies. But if you do here they are:

1. <u>Positioning is more important than it seems</u>: I really recommend you start trying to breastfeed your newborn baby in the Cross-Cradle Position. Remember this position is ideal for babies who need help latching, or are small or premature. To do so, lie your baby on a nursing pillow on your lap. If you are nursing on the left side, cradle your baby's head in your right hand, by placing your thumb by one ear and your forefinger by the other one. Your baby's neck should be supported by the space between the forefinger and the thumb. Allow your palm to

support your baby's upper back and use your left hand to prop up your left breast.

2.   <u>Practical Pacifier Replacement</u>: Clean your hands and insert the tip of your pinky finger in your baby's mouth allowing it to rest gently on the palate. Do this to soothe your baby before breastfeeding and when you feel the suction more subtly replace your finger with your breast.

3.   <u>Correct latch</u>: With one breast in one hand and the baby's back supported in the other one, bring your baby (not just the head, but the whole body) close enough so they can easily reach your nipple. Tickle their upper lip with your nipple, and when your baby opens the mouth wide, use your right hand to push the baby's back toward the breast to get a deep latch. Your baby's chin should touch the breast first and they should latch onto more breast tissue under the nipple than above it.

Your baby's lips should be fully flanged like fish lips and should wrap around your areola. Make sure nothing is blocking your baby's nose and voila!

4. <u>Get comfortable whilst breastfeeding</u>: Support yourself and your baby with pillows so that you aren't hunched over.

5. <u>Relax</u>: Try not to be tense and nervous and really try your best to relax by listening to a playlist, visualising your happy place, taking a few slow, deep breaths and opting for a change of environment.

6. Enjoy periods of cuddling skin-to-skin with your baby.

7. <u>If you do get sore or cracked nipples</u>:
   a. Pump milk so you can regulate the suction intensity.

b. Apply freshly expressed breast milk and a medical grade Lanolin ointment.

c. Use warm compresses and salt water rinses.

d. Let your breasts breathe and air dry as much as possible.

e. Use nipple shields to give your nipples some relief whilst your baby feeds.

f. Buy a couple of milk collection cups and hold them over your nipples or put them inside your bra to save some breast milk.

Acknowledgments

First of all I would like to thank Mia for coming into my life and showing me how much love I have to give and for teaching me how to be the best mum I can be.

My husband for helping me create and bring into this world such a beautiful baby girl, inside and out. He is my rock and is always by my side supporting me in whatever project I want to start and pushing me into believing I got what it takes to be anything I want to be.

My own and my husband's family for being a source of advice, help and more importantly a foundation on which we can trust and build our own.

I can't begin to think this book is finalised without thanking my lactation consultant, who I named Elsie to preserve her identity. Without her, I would have given up on breastfeeding completely and I would have always felt a bit down about it.

My friends and sister-in-law, who were open enough to talk about uncomfortable topics perhaps, but didn't hold back because they knew how important it is to be prepared and have real conversations about something that affects many people and is very little spoken of.

I am eternally grateful to my father, Brian Coulthard, for editing this book and helping me make my words more clear to you. Daddy, thank you for reading this journal a thousand times and for all the constructive criticism you provided. Publishing this book wouldn't have been possible without your help.

My sincere thanks to Surangi, my brother, my husband, Sophie and Julian Cappelli for proofreading this book and their advice.

I am also very thankful to my dear friend Theepa not only for proofreading this memoir but also for helping me convey to the artist what I envisioned for the illustrations in this book.

Heartfelt thanks to A. T. Selvakumaran for capturing what I wanted, designing the images in this book and his beautiful illustrations of Mia and me. Muunaa you truly are an amazing artist.

Last but not least, there is a saying that goes "It takes a village to raise a child" which is very true. But after writing this memoir, I believe it also takes a village to write a book so I would like to thank everyone who in one way or another contributed to this work being finalised.

References

☐ Ag, M. (2021, November 24). Breastfeeding in the first month: What to expect. Medela. Retrieved December 29, 2021, from https://www.medela.com/breastfeeding/mums-journey/support-first-month

☐ Breathnach, T. (2020, January 6). Mixed breast and bottle feeding: how to make it work. MadeForMums. Retrieved January 23, 2022, from https://www.madeformums.com/baby/mixed-feeding-how-to-make-it-work-successfully/

☐ Centers for Disease Control and Prevention. (2021, August 10). Breastfeeding is the best source of nutrition for most infants. Retrieved December 10, 2021, from https://www.cdc.gov/breastfeeding/about-breastfeeding/index.html

☐ Cleveland Clinic. (2021, December 27). Yes, Postpartum Depression in Men Is Very Real. Retrieved January 15, 2022, from https://health.clevelandclinic.org/yes-postpartum-depression-in-men-is-very-real/

☐ Hays, Director Of The Pediatric Clinical Nutrition Education & Practice, T. (2019, July 26). Feeding Guide for the First Year. Johns Hopkins Medicine. Retrieved January 12, 2022, from https://www.hopkinsmedicine.org/health/wellness-and-prevention/feeding-guide-for-the-first-year

☐ Howland, G. (2020, August 8). Breastfeeding Positions: Have You Tried Them All? Mama Natural. Retrieved August 15, 2021 from https://www.mamanatural.com/breastfeeding-positions/

☐ Jana, L. A., & Shu, J. (2009, November 19). Practical Pacifier Principles. HealthyChildren.Org. Retrieved August 26, 2021, from https://www.healthychildren.org/English/ages-stages/baby/crying-colic/Pages/Practical-Pacifier-Principles.aspx

☐ Kiefer, V. A. P. B. A. (2018, April 4). Let's Face It: Formula-Fed Babies Sleep Better. Expecting Science. Retrieved

February 1, 2022, from

https://expectingscience.com/2014/09/09/lets-face-it-

formula-fed-babies-sleep-better-from-their-parents-

perspective/

☐ Murkoff, H. (2016). What to Expect When You're Expecting

(5th ed.). Workman Publishing.

☐ Mustela USA. (2017, August 3). The 12 Best Breastfeeding

Tips For New Mothers. Retrieved November 15, 2021, from

https://www.mustelausa.com/blogs/mustela-mag/the-12-

best-breastfeeding-tips-for-new-mothers

☐ NHS website. (2021, November 18). Breastfeeding: the first

few days. Nhs.Uk. Retrieved December 23, 2021, from

https://www.nhs.uk/conditions/baby/breastfeeding-and-

bottle-feeding/breastfeeding/the-first-few-days/

☐ World Health Organisation. (2019, November 11).

Breastfeeding. WHO - Breastfeeding. Retrieved November

10, 2020, from https://www.who.int/health-

topics/breastfeeding#tab=tab_1

Printed in Great Britain
by Amazon

18344927R00061